YOUR KNOWLEDGE I

- We will publish your bachelor's and master's thesis, essays and papers

- Your own eBook and book - sold worldwide in all relevant shops

- Earn money with each sale

Upload your text at www.GRIN.com and publish for free

The Role of Social Media and the Effectiveness of Communication in HIV and AIDS Prevention

Razlan Rauf

Bibliographic information published by the German National Library:

The German National Library lists this publication in the National Bibliography; detailed bibliographic data are available on the Internet at http://dnb.dnb.de.

ISBN: 9783346905437
This book is also available as an ebook.

Print and binding: Books on Demand GmbH, Norderstedt, Germany
Printed on acid-free paper from responsible sources.

The present work has been carefully prepared. Nevertheless, authors and publishers do not incur liability for the correctness of information, notes, links and advice as well as any printing errors.

GRIN web shop: https://www.grin.com/document/1371216

The Role of Social Media and the Effectiveness of Communication
Design Framework in HIV/Aids Prevention

Razlan Bin Abd Rauf

A research report submitted in partial fulfilment of requirement of the
Master of Communication (Integrated Marketing Communication)

Universiti Sains Malaysia

A research report submitted in partial fulfilment of requirement of the

Master of Communication (Integrated Marketing Communication)

School of Communication
Universiti Sains Malaysia
April 2021

TABLE OF CONTENT

LIST OF FIGURES

ABSTRACT

The first cases of HIV in Malaysia were reported in 1986, and there was a sharp increase in 10 cases by 1990. After scientists introduced three combinations of Antiretroviral (ART) treatments in 1995, there was a decrease in the HIV cases. In 2018, the rate of new HIV cases in Malaysia was 10 cases per 100,000 population. Of these cases, a total of 47 patients involved individuals under the age of 18. No treatment can eliminate the virus as a whole, but HIV can be prevented or given early treatment before the onset of AIDS. So, early detection and safety precaution to avoid being infected by the disease is essential. Social media has essentially changed how people communicate and share information (Kaplan & Haenlein, 2009), and health communication has indeed been immune to this information revolution (Kreps, 2011). With the advent of Facebook, people, without having to meet, can interact with each other. Nowadays, many new media facilities such as the internet, smartphones, and others have given society a new dimension in understanding HIV / AIDS and its actions. There is very little research on public awareness of HIV / AIDS and the role played by social media in dealing with this disease. This study aim to explore the predictive part of social media use on public preventive behaviours and how the disease knowledge and eHealth literacy moderated the relationship between social media use and preventive behaviours on HIV/ AIDS in Malaysia contexts. A proportionate probability sampling conducted an online cross-sectional survey among social media users in Malaysia. The participants will complete the questionnaires based on designated areas of interest on social media on HIV/ AIDS. Methods on descriptive statistics, Pearson correlations, and hierarchical multiple regressions will be used to examine and explore the relationships among all the variables.

CHAPTER 1

INTRODUCTION

1.0   Background

Nowadays, many new media facilities such as the internet, smartphones, and others have given society a new dimension in understanding HIV / AIDS and its actions. Previously, only traditional media such as television, radio and newspapers provided information about HIV / AIDS to the community. The internet allows such issues to be collected, communicated and discussed openly with the public. Indirectly, it affects public awareness of the dangers of this disease. There is very little research on public awareness of HIV / AIDS and the role played by social media in dealing with this disease. The level of public awareness and knowledge on HIV issues is deficient. Community involvement in understanding and addressing the issue of HIV / AIDS is still low. Whether a person feels close to those living with HIV / AIDS or not, they are interdependent and need each other in whatever daily activities they go through (Tan Pei San & Norzaini, 2011).

Based on Maibach, Bonaguro and Kreps (1993, p.15-35) practical HIV/AIDS prevention strategies "...must begin with careful campaign planning in which campaign objectives are decided, the goal audience's particular requirements orientations examined, and the target audience segmented into homogeneous organizations. The communication method must be thoroughly analyzed to determine effective and accessible communication channels, design plan communications, and test these messages for use with target audiences. The final requirement is that the campaign outcomes should be thoroughly evaluated; to identify probable influences of the campaign on overall health behaviours as well as instructions of future risk avoidance and wellness communication endeavours might be identified."

Social media's advancement allows users to easily share information and tell stories or news through blogs, social networks, or forums in the virtual world. This internet is an integral part of influencing the daily life of a person in this generation 4.0. Almost every detail of our daily lives needs internet technology and social media to purchase daily necessities, interact with others, and generate income. Based on the chart of social media use by citizens world, Malaysian society has broken the record of the highest place in the world in using social applications such as WhatsApp and Facebook due to sophistication that can record live video with other users. Social media's rapid development is now a factor because all the world's population can afford to own a smartphone (Nadia Fauzi, 2017).

Social media has essentially changed how people communicate and share information (Kaplan & Haenlein, 2009), and health communication has indeed been immune to this information revolution (Kreps, 2011). As social media's general use expands, research related to social media use for health communication purposes also increases in scope (Moorhead, Hazlett, Harrison, Carroll, Irwin & Hoving, 2013). Social media is the essential tool or instrument used to convey information, build perceptions, and shape public attitudes about the data presented. The media has proven to be a vital tool or intermediary in communicating certain information and messages. The media's importance focus to convey information but more than that because the media plays a role in shaping society's thinking patterns.

Therefore, through today's social media technology, all information is readily available without borders, time and limits—Similarly, information related to official affairs, news, health and awareness about the environment. However, information disseminated through the internet differs in technique from information published in newspapers or notices on signboards. Those who provide information should count on current trends that require readers to read concisely. It does not need a long description because netizens want to save time and want to know briefly (Todd, 2018). Information and communication through the internet must have a design that is in line with the changes in the 4.0 era commonly detailed yet simple. The scope of this study involves the role of social media in HIV and AIDS communication. Social media's essential in

3

ensuring that people know and acquire knowledge of relevant content about HIV and AIDS not to be stuck with ignorance that will cause them to infected with the disease.

Communication design is an essential aspect of communication in conveying information to readers on the internet. Another opinion says communication design is an activity to transform something innovative and make something useful through creative images (Mark, 2007). The informant's responsibility is to design the best type of information display to convey the message to netizens easily. The communication designer is responsible for connecting the communication in the form of a message through a clear vision for the reader to get the information.

To ensure that the reader gets a visual display of the information, a communication designer will consider the message conveyed and ensure how the message can be transferred to the reader directly, clearly and easily. This aspect is essential to ensure that the information reaches the reader. Communication designers will formulate strategies and plans before designing the visual space to consider what attracts the reader's attention first (Lucy Todd, 2018). From the aspect of sentence structure, pictures, font application and some elements in the display of information. All these communication designs must consider the reader's perspective to understand or otherwise present data to disseminate. The design arrangement is different and not the same according to the designer's taste (Clare, 2019). Therefore, the element that takes into account is whether the reader understands the message to be conveyed or not, not according to the designer's wishes but according to the reader's wishes following time 4.0 (John, 2017).

Hence, the designer will consider what attracts the audience, the general interaction, and the psychological perspective behind how the design elements affect the reader's feelings, emotions, and mind while reading the information (Clare, 2019). Through previous studies, communication design defines simpler and simpler visuals to express information strategically

4

(Gwen et al., 2018). Compared to the advancement of information technology today, graphic design is changing and better quality than before to make the visuals more competitive among fellow designers.

1.1 Research Objective

This study aim to explore the predictive role of social media use on public preventive behaviours and how the disease knowledge and eHealth literacy moderate the relationship between social media use and preventive behaviours on HIV/ AIDS in Malaysia contexts. Specifically, it appraises the effect of social media tools via the mass media on the HIV and AIDS in Malaysia.

The secondary goal is assessing the perceived advantages and limitations of utilizing social networking for HIV and AIDS communication. To think about how to use social networking for health-related communication, and more particularly HIV/AIDS communication, advertising practitioners have to note which factors contribute to which elements and effective communication hinder communication.

1.2 Research Question 1:

Does social media use is predictive of public behaviours among Malaysia social media user in HIV and AIDS?

1.3 Research Question 2:

Do social media types (official social media, professional social media, public social media, and aggregated social media) differ in predicting one's preventive behaviours in HIV/AIDS?

1.4 Research Question 3:

Does disease knowledge and eHealth literacy moderates the relationship between social media use and public preventive behaviour?

1.5 Research Scope and Significance

Research Scope: The Use of Social Media and Preventive Behaviours

In producing this study, the researcher has determined that this study will include all respondents who use social media as the primary, intermediate relationship or communication in their daily activities.

The way people communicate has changed over the past years. Most of us are spending more times with social media. Social media design helps in facilitating the communication process and social interaction among people. Moreover, most of the public health response become the immediacy of the social media application. General-purpose social networking like Facebook offers the opportunity to the normative pathway to reach prevention of particular behaviours. Moreover, Facebook, which has a broader audience, focuses not only on social relationship but also on preventive behaviours towards HIV/ AIDS. The underlying mechanism on social media use to behavioural health change is that the scope of HIV/ AIDS on social media could increase the public's fear and direct them to take preventive behaviours. Process of communication via social media engage with the communication exchanges in terms of semantic features of interaction, such as revealing clues about interest, norms, and willingness to engage in preventive and risk behaviours.

The individual will be a cluster in social media relationships like friendship and group of affiliation. It will be focusing on the behaviours enforcement among others upon the link to the network in which individual will share certain behavioural traits. Generally, the social media network's goals will establish a connection between how people "talk" and deliver idea on social media that influence people to engage in preventive behaviours. Communication in social media will lead to prevention risk behaviour. Moreover, it will link what people talk about and the actual conduct on the prevention of HIV/ AIDS.

This study's underlying factor, based on infectious diseases in this era of modernity, is increasing in the health sector since the early 90s. The government and several organisations involved in medicine and healthcare worldwide have devised a strategic plan to deal with infectious diseases, especially HIV and AIDS, among Malaysians. According to the World Health Organization (WHO), this plan develops and expanded on debates and strategy statistics according to the World Health Organization (WHO) based on established guidelines including strategies or action plans to deal with the disease, the response from viruses' recovery from those diseases. Emerging infectious diseases have a broad definition covering diseases such as previously unknown AIDS, Ebola, recurrent infections such as tuberculosis, measles, pertussis, existing diseases that have moved to new places of the West Nile virus, hepatitis. Conditions can no longer under controlled by highly effective drugs such as malaria and illnesses that show an increase in virulence, such as the COVID-19 Pandemic Virus (Dr Risma, 2020). The disease's emergence includes several important aspects, including an increase in the world's population, population density in Municipal areas with poor hygiene, provision of unclean food and beverages, and excessive use of drugs such as antibiotics.

Other scholars argue that designing an effective communication design is essential in facing challenges such as declining public awareness of HIV and AIDS. The show is done from hand or television distribution to digital or various website sources to get the latest information (Collins et al., 1999). Furthermore, the emergence of viruses and bacteria through HIV and AIDS has led to the expansion of communication and multimedia in the health sector in general. Therefore, through this study, the researcher found that the problems in disseminating information in social media are practical or otherwise through the design of the communication conducted. The extent to which the effect occurs, the dissemination made and the number of netizens aware of the information.

Furthermore, in the communication of information regarding HIV and AIDS, the researcher has emphasised several vital aspects, namely understanding the target audience, planning effectively on the message or data to be disseminated to suit the target audience. The information communication management needs to consider resources or channels accepted and have official certainty, such as direct information. The study adopt a model by Li & Liu, 2020, on Social Media Use, eHealth Literacy, Disease Knowledge, and Preventive Behaviors in COVID-19 Pandemic: A Cross-Sectional Study on Chinese Netizens which predicted public preventive behaviours during COVID-19 outbreak in Chinese contexts.

CHAPTER 2

LITERATURE REVIEW

2.0   Definition of Social Media and Subject Matter Focus

Many companies or news take this platform as it is easy to access at flexible times. Furthermore, individuals can choose their own free time to read the information without waiting or missing data. Social media can also provide advantages or support in features or tools that allow the company or person to disseminate information to other netizens based on keywords or fields of interest based on what people might search on the internet (Andreas, 2010).

a)   Role of Social Media in Information Seeking and Delivery

Social media is one of the internet technologies that all the people of the world actively use to obtain information, disseminate information and verify the authenticity of the data presented. Based on previous studies, they use the uses-and gratification approach to research and analyse the study results to the extent of the user's personality in filtering the information sought on Facebook. A study in Germany with 1525 Facebook users participated in this study. It mainly confirms the filtering of information through 3 types of properties, extraversion, neuroticism and openness as predictors in the block-wise regression model. The researcher stated that the censorship made by a person when searching for information on social media depends on the behaviour of the individual. If the individual is positive thinking and can receive the data, the data is accepted positively (Kai Kaspar, 2019). If censorship in seeking information has not done, it can cause dire implications such as slander, and the information does not reach the user, etc.

b)   Role of Social Media in Persuasion

The meaning discussed by the past review in their study uses social media for visual persuasion in propagating the establishment to change individual perceptions of something and

9

information towards what the researcher wants to base on the study's objectives (Hew Wai Weng, 2018). Hence, social media can openly shape the audience's thoughts and turn those thoughts into a desire to start a protest or action together. Social media allows individuals to disseminate information creatively and attract the public's attention through various text, visuals, and videos. Social media information dissemination aims to invite netizens to be aware and alert with that information and indirectly convince them to change the habit from the worst to a healthy lifestyle. Foucault discussed this process in detail, a normalization method that indirectly carries the meaning of effort to invite and persuade others. It does not force directly in a state of softness and build awareness spontaneously. Relaxed mood until the individual is convinced and can receive the information (cited by Hew Wai Weng, 2018). Thus, giving a positive result can influence the individual's thinking and enable the individual to disseminate the thought or information to the closest contacts in a chain using social media (Ran Huang et al., 2017).

2.1 Subject Matter Focus: HIV and AIDS

HIV stands for human immunodeficiency virus, which acts to cause harm to the human immune system by damaging the white blood cells that function to prevent and kill infections in the human body. It makes the human body vulnerable to various viruses and cancers easily. At the same time, AIDS is the final stage of HIV found by only a small number of patients with HIV. AIDS stands for acquired immunodeficiency syndrome (Susan, 2020). The growth of technology mediated-communication platforms, like social media, is essential in the modification of contemplating. They provide the potential of disseminating tailored wellness communications to entirely strongly defined organizations (Chou, Hunt, Beckjord, Moser, & Hesse, 2009). Nevertheless, the effect of social networking within the context of HIV/AIDS specific communication, and the consequent challenges for interaction approach advancement, appear still reasonably unexplored.

As the connection between technology and business for overall health is rapidly developing, Venkateswaran (2011) argues that sociable media's energy for health communication is becoming more apparent.

2.2 Theories and Model Framework

According to Social Cognitive Theory, human being learns behaviours via observation, modelling and motivation. In this theory, people will learn from others from now and then. Among the two ways of learning, behaviours are direct experience and observations of others. It encompasses four processes such as attention, retention, motor reproduction and reinforcement and motivation. Triadic reciprocal determinism influences the individual cognitive that affect other behaviour. An individual with internal competencies of mental, emotional and physical will learn from the environment as the external factors that result in behaviour that lead to action and decision. In this study, social media affects people cognitively as their internal competencies that later direct those to specific behaviour on the move or decision. According to Lin & Chang, 2018, Social Cognitive Theory emphasizes that human behaviour is shaped and controlled by personal cognition in a social environment. Bandura further proposes two types of expectation beliefs, such as outcome expectations and self-efficacy, and suggests that they are the two major cognitive forces that will guide an individual's behaviour.

Social media tools design continuously make people addicted to it. It will capture as much as peoples' attention on it used. The attention drives people towards addictive behaviour on social media usage as they would like to know what is happening in the world. For example, when people post about the potential behaviour risk of HIV and AIDS on social media that appear on other people's news feed as it is frequently appearing. This social media technology will help people change their state of consciousness to preventive behaviours of HIV and AIDS.

11

Reviewing the information posted on social media as Facebook will interfere with the medium and long-term preventative action goals. The information has to be something important that engage with human cognition, such as the importance of preventive behaviour of HIV and AIDS.

2.3 Health Literacy and Preventive Behaviours

Social media's internal assets become the predictors of preventive measures, including knowledge about the health, capabilities, and skills employed, known as "Health Literacy". The attribute of health literacy becomes essential for predicting health promotion and prevention. According to centres for disease control and prevention, personal health literacy is the degree to which individuals can find, understand, and use information and services to inform themselves and others' health-related decisions and actions (Dr. Rudd, 2021). This health literacy framework develops as people nowadays seek out, apprehend, value, and utilise any health information.

Social media is a platform that connects communication between individuals through the technology of unlimited internet use and boundaries. This platform acts as an interactive field in sharing information, ideas, and reference materials for selected individuals or audiences to note that information and up to date with the latest news (Obar and Wildman, 2015). Electronic health (eHealth) literacy is the combination between media and information literacies which later applied under eHealth publicity. Therefore, information on social media filtered according to the individual's wishes and criteria is seeking health information for the purpose. The information sought gives functional implications to users. eHealth literacy positively engages people with health problem such as HIV and AIDS in maintaining their health status lead to quality of life.

2.4   Definition of Communication Design Framework

The display seen in each banner, poster, or advertisement digitally is an information element to send the message to humans to process the information and understand what conveyed. The human brain will receive every news said, and if the message has something to do with itself, then the message is considered successful and absorbed into the mind (Aditya Johri, 2012). However, if the passage's communication is irrelevant because the elements of differences in understanding individuals, such as differences in language, information, and others, can cause the message sent is not successful and not absorbed into the mind.

The individual will ignore the information presented by displaying information on banners, posters or digital advertisements if the information presented is not successful (WHO, 2017). Therefore, the designer should design a design that can convey the target audience's information or goal in giving any emotion or impact relevant to the audience. This channel is known as the Communication Design Framework, which is a communication framework. It involves relationships between individuals and topics presented through a framework that attracts the individual's attention. As a result, it can affect the individual's beliefs, concepts, values or behaviour from not paying attention to the topic presented to give full attention (Airhihenbuwa, 1999). Therefore, every design made to get positive feedback and high engagement from the target audience, hoping that the individual can influence them to show interest in a given topic.

a)   Communication Design in Information Seeking and Delivery

Communication is a critical element that will influence the individual's thoughts and behaviours based on the delivery of the first individual to the second individual. The intended delivery method is an appropriate technique to control a person to believe the message he wants to convey. Even getting support from many the target audience, publicity, or broadcast is the best way to share the desired news (Maria Louisa, 2018). Techniques or designs created following the audience's thoughts or areas of interest so that the message conveyed successfully influences their behaviour and invites others such as close acquaintances to support and arouse interest in the source of information. It means that the communication design can provide information or a platform for those who want to find information in detail. The audience begins to feel confident in the information source and seek advice in this domain (Maria Louisa, 2018).

Previous researchers have stated that all types of design are responsive and have a text that can influence individual thinking (Maria Louisa, 2018), yet so has the extent to which the reader or display can influence individual thinking. In other words, the individual may take note and understand the message that the ad display wants to convey. However, most likely, it cannot influence the individual to cause changes in individual behaviour after reading the ad or campaign.

The display made maybe just a weak interaction to increase the audience engagement rate. However, some advertising displays can cause an individual influence if communication is effective (cited by Maria Louisa, 2018). Therefore, the display's information makes it an essential element for the individual to continue seeking that information through legit sources or people who send the message as discussed by the media sector or designer in an organisation to produce an effective design communication (Keshab R. Acharya, 2017).

b)   Communication Design in Persuasion

Apart from seeking information and transmitting information, communication design acts as an element of persuasion in changing individuals' thoughts or behaviours from passive to active in supporting or showing interest in a featured topic. Other opinions state that any message in the form of narrative and displayed through proper communication design can effectively impact the audience's emotions (Fuyuan Shen, 2015). Not only that, but communication carried out interpersonal or campaign more persuasive towards the social change of society because they are more emotionally attracted or messages delivered face to face without digital display or printed text (Emily Acosta, 2013). Therefore, persuasion in communication design is essential to get positive value to the communication effect presented. It can avoid problems such as lack of information or misunderstanding if the plan is detailed and follows the target audience's norms (Shaddin et al., 2016).

2.5 Hypotheses

The study's key concept refers to media, which comprises measurements, the research questions on media usage, and health behaviours that people spend on social media every day. Another, the frequency of using the social media platform such as Facebook, YouTube, Instagram, then will be summarized based on the "period of using the media" (for example, hours spend) and the number of times media use (recurrence). Hence. "Time" and "Frequency" known as the variables of social media use. Two hypotheses generated as per below:

Hypothesis 1: Social media use time is positively associated with preventive behaviours in HIV and AIDS.

Hypothesis 2: Social media use frequency is positively associated with preventive behaviours in HIV and AIDS.

Besides the time and frequency, the type will be another crucial dimension of social media use. By looking at the current media landscape trend that dramatically changes media use within the new media environment and looking at the Malaysia scenario, people receive news of further information through multiple channels such as traditional and online media. Based on the statistic, Facebook's rate-focused in Malaysia from 2017 until 2019 has reached 23 million users across the peninsular, Sabah and Sarawak. The number of Facebook users expected to rise to 25.95 million by the time it comes in 2021 (Statista, 2020). Tobergte, 2010, stated that internet-based applications have significantly reduced the cost to collect, distribute, and access information, save resources, and create new mechanisms in integrating organizations with users together. Social media is the primary channel to improve the information delivery system with users' involvement, such as students actively in development affairs and student activities at the university level. In this regard, it should enhance the social media use among people related to the delivery of information to HIV / AIDS to provide helpful information to all individuals and make social media a sharing platform related to the disease.

In Malaysia, the official media acts as formal information by the government or any government agencies. Professional social media exist based on news and professional domain. For example, Money Matters in TV3 highlighting the topic of the economy. Aggregated social media is a type of media that assemble and segregate news and information by various agencies. It can be on the scope of the economy, sports politics and others, While public social media, known as interpersonal social media that produce and distributes messages on an individual basis.

Moreover, with the distinguishing features based on social media, it brings various effects to the audience. The website-based content will help the audience with safer sex literacy by sharing information via social networking platforms. Traditional media such as newspaper and radio acts as an effective medium with crisis management compared with social media. Meanwhile, social media happen to have an impact on any related intervention with public health. However, the younger generation strongly relies on social media for information seeking. Examining the factors affecting health information exchange could advance our understanding of how to sustain information sharing and information-seeking behaviours in social media and maintain social media success (Lin & Chang, 2018). On the other hand, the designated information or messages transferred via trusted online personal broadcasting. It will be able to direct users' attitudes or intentions to change. Based on previous studies, social media acts as an essential platform for their users to discover social media's potential as the primary source of information exchange, especially Facebook (Kai Kaspar, 2019). Initially, Facebook was a platform for connecting users without borders and time limits. However, Facebook has developed over the years, making it one of the essential sources in accessing various latest information, including knowing current news or posts that involve awareness about things that happen worldwide (Marketa, 2019). William argues that this matter included using social media to seek information, deliver the message, and connect people to gain the amount of information source (cited by Kai Kaspar, 2019).

The combination between the disease knowledge and eHealth literacy associated with health status. As independently related to disease knowledge and eHealth literacy which impact the disease knowledge through the indirect channel. For example, sexual transmitted diseases knowledge known to be contributed information with safe sex protection to prevent HIV and AIDS. As a result, four hypotheses predicted as below:

Hypothesis three: eHealth literacy is positively associated with preventive behaviours in HIV and AIDS.

Hypothesis four: Diseases knowledge is positively associated with preventive behaviours in HIV and AIDS.

Hypothesis five: eHealth literacy moderates the relationship between social media use and preventive behaviours in HIV and AIDS.

Hypothesis six: Disease knowledge moderates the relationship between social media use and preventive behaviours in HIV and AIDS.

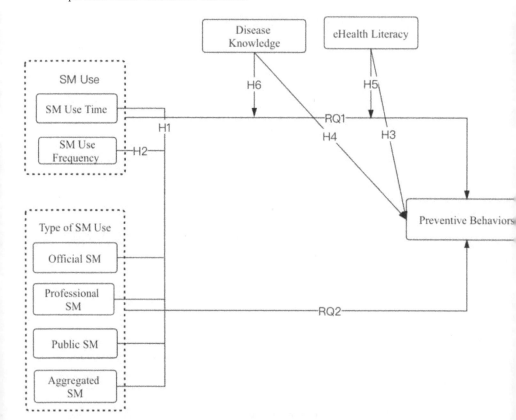

Figure 1. A framework map of the research questions and hypotheses.

CHAPTER 3

RESEARCH METHODOLOGY

3.0 Research Methods and Research Design

Research Methods

Research Methodology is a scientific knowledge that studies the ways of doing observations with complete, precise thinking through the stages scientifically compiled to find, calculate, compile and analyse and summarise the data so that can use it to discover, develop and test the truth of knowledge (Creswell, 2013). Knowledge learned using the correct procedure and accurate methods through searching, calculating, organising information and analysing information. Thus, the study can formulate to collect data to produce new idea and knowledge. Furthermore, this research method is a procedure or steps to gain scientific expertise or build a systematic study and be understood by researchers and other communities (Marvasti, 2018). So the research conducted is a systematic way to compile the research technique to implement the method. The data results are legit and used by other researchers as a reference through correct steps. Several other communities can understand the research methods as a source of concern for the research methods implemented. Research methodology can positively impact researchers and other readers alike (Marvasti, 2018). Thus, the use of correct and appropriate study methods is essential to avoid confusion throughout the study.

Research Design

This study will use quantitative methods on cross-sectional, survey-based design to obtain clear and solid information for the specified variables. The use of quantitative methods in this study will assign a value to each measurement unit, whether it is more, less or the exact value according to the variable (Creswell, 2013). Besides, measurements made according to the correlation between the variables.

Correlation is a statistical reading that explains the relationship between two variables, whether the variables have similar values to each other or vice versa. The correlation value is determined by reading the number 0.1 and above. If the reading shows a negative 0.1, then the value is an error or does not correlate (Chen & Popovich, 2011).

3.1 Demographic Information

Among the socio-demographic variables in this study consist of gender (male and female), age (18-30, 30-40, 40 above), level of education (SPM, Degree, Master and Doctorate), and household income (RM 1000 and below, RM1000 to RM2000, RM2000 to RM3000, RM3000 to RM4000 and RM5000 above). Besides, marital status (single, married and divorced), health status (healthy or comorbidities) and location (Klang Valley Malaysia).

3.2 Methods

Design and Recruitment

The study will employ an online cross-sectional survey that applied proportionate probability sampling methods to examine whether social media usage predicted Malaysian social media users' preventive behaviours on HIV and AIDS. Besides, it will use as the moderators of disease knowledge and eHealth literacy. The proportionate sampling method applies based on the distribution of gender and age Malaysia social media user, internet. The sample selected for this study is purposive sampling, a selection that selects specific respondents to obtain effective study results. Purposive sampling use as representative of the study population as a whole. Therefore, the sampling technique used is according to the Tabachnick and Fidell sampling technique (Tabachnick & Fidell, 2012). The Tabachnick and Fidell sampling technique is a formula based on specific respondent values and represents a population.

The formula is as below:-

$$N = > 50 + 8 \ (m)$$

$$N = > 50 + 8 \ (6)$$

$$N = > 50 + 48$$

$$N = > 98$$

N = appropriate sample size

m = the number of independent variables

Therefore, the number of sampling used in this research is 98 samples and above to provide reliable correlations.

Participants in this study will be using the online designated Google Survey Form based on the relevance to the executed variable. The questionnaire developed, and a pilot study will be deploy to selected participants.

3.3 Instruments

- **Social Media Use**

Media is a tool and a medium of communication, intermediary or liaison. While social means community or imaginary. Among the popular social media at the moment is Mark Zuckerberg, who founded Facebook focused. In term of media use, it will be measured based on the questions such as 1) social media use time (on the previous week, how long do you use social media to search information about HIV/ AIDS? The time set range from less than an hour, 5 hours or more than 5 hours.

On the other hand, social media use refers to the most frequent channel used to seek information about HIV and AIDS in everyday life. As explained before, the four types of social media channels known as official social media, for example, The Star Malaysia mobile and professional social media such as 'doctor on call'. Another, public social media such as Facebook, aggregated social media such as Utusan Malaysia. It ranges from 1: never used, 2:

21

1-2 times per week, 3: 3-4 times per week, 4: 5-6 times per week, 5: more than one time per day. Moreover, measured social media used frequency based on the frequency's total score on all social media channels. Whenever the respondent attained more score, it means that social media used frequently.

• **Preventive Behaviours**

In terms of aspects of preventive behaviours, the items measured based on World Health Organization's basic recommendations include practising safe sex while involving intercourse, using protection such as condoms, and avoiding sharing drugs abuse by sharing a needle. The study by Beeker, Guenther-Grey, & Raj, 1998, emphasizes two recently completed multi-site HIV prevention intervention studies funded through the Centers for Disease Control and Prevention (CDC) also exemplify paradigm drift. The AIDS Community Demonstration Projects and the Prevention of HIV in Women and Infants Demonstration Projects (WIDP) enlisted populations at risk for HIV. It uses to deliver community-relevant HIV-prevention messages and condoms (or bleach kits for injecting drug users) to their peers and provide social support for behaviour change (O'Reilly and Higgins, 1991; CDC, 1996). All the relevant items later will be assessed on self-development measurement. According to the World Health Organisation (WHO), the disease knowledge measures based on World Health Organisation (WHO) campaign on HIV and AIDS.

On the other hand, as per preventive measure promoted by the Ministry of Health Malaysia. A pilot study conducted mainly to determine the validity and reliability before being accepted with the actual survey execution. All the respondents involved in the survey deliver their opinion to contribute to the findings. Their view on what extent they agree with the statements related to the prevention of HIV and AIDS.

- **Disease Knowledge**

Other factors besides eHealth Literacy are disease knowledge that becomes the main elements of health literacy. Disease knowledge will enable people to identify symptoms, cause, and available perceive risks of infectious diseases such as HIV and AIDS. Once people have a better understanding of the disease knowledge, it will enable them by improving the quality of health management as prevention to HIV and AIDS. It will be the predictor to change one's health behaviours. Ministry of Health, Malaysia, targets 90% of HIV treatment coverage by 2020. No treatment can eliminate the virus as a whole, but HIV can be prevented or given early treatment before the onset of AIDS. So, early detection and safety precaution to avoid being infected by the disease is vital. Hence, the Ministry of Health will implement relevant safety measures to enhance the public's understanding of disease knowledge that focuses on altering the public's traits and behaviours via public health prevention.

The same assessment will use for disease knowledge using respondent self-development measurement (for example: "Sharing of needle for drug addicts prone to be infected with HIV and AIDS"). The same instrument with preventive measure employ within the study as per guidelines set up by the World Health Organisation (WHO) on prevention of HIV and AIDS. Since the research focuses on the Malaysian context, it will focus on the standard guidelines by the Ministry of Health, Malaysia. A pilot test will also be done to test the questionnaire statement, instruction, and time allocation. For will give each correct answer given by participants will be given a score on each item. Disease knowledge according to the score of 0-10 (Cronbach's alpha $\alpha = 10$). Moreover, it will report on the reliability and validity of the questionnaire.

eHealth Literacy

This variable assessed one's perceived ability to seek, understand, and appraise health information on HIV and AIDS disease, and the participants apply the knowledge indicate on any related health concerns. Malaysia National eHealth focuses on being a nation of healthy individuals, families and communities. Among the eight goals, Malaysia National eHealth such as wellness focus, person focus, informed persons, self-help, care provided at home/close to home, seamless, continuous care, services tailored as much as possible, effective, efficient and affordable services (Shaik Allaudin, 2008). The questionnaire on this being developed in English which associated with the prevention of HIV and AIDS. The available options will be using a 5-point Likert scale that ranges from "1 = disagree" up to "5 = agree".

3.4 Statistical Analysis

The socio-demographic analysis will be using descriptive statistics such as gender, age, level of education, household income, marital status, health status, and locality. These are the category variables on the category variables described based on count and percentage, which will then be dummy coded and set one group as a reference group. Pearson correlations analysis and hierarchical multiple regressions will use for this study. It examines the correlation between control variables and independent variables and dependent variables; meanwhile, the mean and standard deviation used to analyse the continuous variables.

The study also uses the methods on two hierarchical regression models that test the research questions and hypotheses. For the first hierarchical multiple regression, the study investigates Research Question 1, Hypothesis 1, Hypothesis 2, Hypothesis 3, Hypothesis 4, Hypothesis 5, and Hypothesis 6. Here, demographics set as the control variables for Model 1. Moreover, the social media use time and social media use frequency introduced in Model 2. Next, the disease knowledge and eHealth literacy introduced in Model 3. The last measurement will be on two interaction items of social media use frequency multiply to disease knowledge, and social media use frequency multiplies to eHealth literacy inserted in Model 4. The other two interactions items of use frequency eHealth literacy and multiply disease knowledge included in Model 5. The second hierarchical regression deploys a deeper examination of four social media types' predictors, research question 2. In Model 1, the demographics set as control variables and four social media types such as official social media, professional social media, public social media, aggregated social media applied in Model 2.

3.5   Data Collection

The data collection process is conducted through random survey questionnaires and according to the researcher's characteristics in the study's scope. The questionnaire will be designed and distributed through Google Forms online to make it easier for respondents to answer the questionnaire. Besides, it can save time and cost of distributing the questionnaire. The sample will be analysed using SPSS software to obtain accurate study data.

3.6 Measurement of Studies

The instrument used to carry out this study is through questions research digitally. This method is suitable for the process of data collection through quantitative requiring accurate data. Moreover, this study concealing the identity of the respondent involved.

REFERENCES

Aakhus, M. (2007). Communication as design. *Communication Monographs, 74*(1), 112-117. https://doi.org/10.1080/03637750701196383

Baulch, E., Watkins, J., & Tariq, A. (2017). *MHealth innovation in Asia: Grassroots challenges and practical interventions.* Springer.

Beeker, C., Guenther-Grey, C., & Raj, A. (1998). Community empowerment paradigm drift and the primary prevention of HIV/AIDS. *Social Science and Medicine, 46*(7), 831–842. https://doi.org/10.1016/S0277-9536(97)00208-6

Chou, W. Y. S., Hunt, Y. M., Beckjord, E. B., Moser, R. P., & Hesse, B. W. (2009). Social media use in the United States: Implications for health communication. *Journal of Medical Internet Research, 11*(4). https://doi.org/10.2196/jmir.1249

Lin, H. C., & Chang, C. M. (2018). What motivates health information exchange in social media? The roles of the social cognitive theory and perceived interactivity. *Information and Management, 55*(6), 771–780. https://doi.org/10.1016/j.im.2018.03.006

Brown, J. D. (2002). The Cronbach alpha reliability estimate. *Shiken: JALT Testing & Evaluation SIG Newsletter.*

Cann, a, Dimitriou, K., Hooley, T., & Research Information Network. (2011). Social Media : A guide for researchers. *History.*

Chen, P. Y., & Popovich, P. M. (2011). Correlation: Parametric And Nonparametric Measures. In *correlation.* https://doi.org/10.4135/9781412983808.n1

Chou, W. Y. S., Hunt, Y. M., Beckjord, E. B., Moser, R. P., & Hesse, B. W. (2009). Social media use in the United States: Implications for health communication. *Journal of Medical Internet Research, 11*(4). https://doi.org/10.2196/jmir.1249

Clare Terry. (2020, August 27). *What is communication design? Everything you need to know.*

Shillington Design Blog. https://www.shillingtoneducation.com/blog/communication
design Creswell, J. (2013). Qualitative, quantitative, and mixed methods approaches. In
Research design.

Fauzi, N. (2017). Penggunaan Media Sosial Dalam Dunia Tanpa Sempadan: Suatu Kebaikan
Atau Keburukan?. Penggunaan Media Sosial Dalam Dunia Tanpa Sempadan: Suatu
Kebaikan Atau Keburukan? , 1–35. Retrieved from
http://www.ilkap.gov.my/download/kertaspenyelidikan/PMSDDTS18122017.pdf

Emily Acosta Lewis. (2013). Theory and Practice of Persuasion. *Media Studies.*
http://www.semesteratsea.org/wp-content/uploads/2012/05/A-
Lewis_SEMS3500_Persuasion1.pdf

Gary L. Kreps, (2011). The Routledge Handbook of Health Communication: The Influence
of Health Communication Scholarship on Health Policy, Practice, and Outcomes

Gwen Lettis et. al. (2018). Encouraging Responsible design the use of value thinking and
psychology in the education of graphic communication designers. *Iterations, 6.*
https://ulir.ul.ie/bitstream/handle/10344/8515/Lettis_2018_Encouraging.pdf?sequenc
e=2

Hajská, M. (2019). The presentation of social status on a social network: The role of
Facebook among the Vlax Romani community of Eastern-Slovak origin in Leicester,
UK. *Romani Studies, 29*(2), 123-158. https://doi.org/10.3828/rs.2019.6

Holmes, B. J. (2008). Communicating about emerging infectious disease: The importance of
research. *Health, Risk & Society, 10*(4), 349-360.
https://doi.org/10.1080/13698570802166431

27

John Spacey. (2017). *9 types of communication design*. Simplicable. https://simplicable.com/new/communication-design

Johri, A., & Pal, J. (2012). Capable and convivial design (CCD): A framework for designing information and communication technologies for human development. *Information Technology for Development, 18*(1), 61-75. https://doi.org/10.1080/02681102.2011.643202

Kaplan, A. M., & Haenlein, M. (2010). Users of the world, unite! The challenges and opportunities of social media. *Business Horizons, 53*(1), 59-68. https://doi.org/10.1016/j.bushor.2009.09.003

Kaspar, K., & Müller-Jensen, M. (2019). Information seeking behavior on Facebook: The role of censorship endorsement and personality. *Current Psychology*. https://doi.org/10.1007/s12144-019-00316-8

Keesman, K. J. (2011). Correlation methods. In Advanced Textbooks in Control and Signal Processing. https://doi.org/10.1007/978-0-85729-522-4_4

Kenpro. (2012). *Sample Size Determination Using Krejcie and Morgan Table*. Kenya Projects Organization.

Lee, D. K., In, J., & Lee, S. (2015). Standard deviation and standard error of the mean. *Korean Journal of Anesthesiology*. https://doi.org/10.4097/kjae.2015.68.3.220

Beeker, C., Guenther-Grey, C., & Raj, A. (1998). Community empowerment paradigm drift and the primary prevention of HIV/AIDS. *Social Science and Medicine, 46*(7), 831–842. https://doi.org/10.1016/S0277-9536(97)00208-6

Chou, W. Y. S., Hunt, Y. M., Beckjord, E. B., Moser, R. P., & Hesse, B. W. (2009). Social media use in the United States: Implications for health communication. *Journal of*

28

Medical Internet Research, 11(4). https://doi.org/10.2196/jmir.1249

Lin, H. C., & Chang, C. M. (2018). What motivates health information exchange in social

media? The roles of the social cognitive theory and perceived interactivity. *Information*

and Management, 55(6), 771–780. https://doi.org/10.1016/j.im.2018.03.006

Lucy Todd. (2018, October 23). *Communication design: The complexity of simplicity*. Killer

Visual Strategies. https://killervisualstrategies.com/blog/communication-design-the

complexity-of-simplicity.html

Maibach, E.W., Kreps, G.L. and Bonaguro, E.W. (1993) Developing Strategic

Communication Campaigns for HIV/AIDS Prevention. In: Ratzan, S.C., Ed., AIDS:

Effective Health Communication for the 90s, Taylor & Francis, Washington, DC, 15-

35.

Marvasti, A. (2018). Research methods. In *The Cambridge Handbook of Social Problems*.

https://doi.org/10.1017/9781108656184.003

Moorhead SA, Hazlett DE, Harrison L, Carroll JK, Irwin A, Hoving C. (2013) A new

dimension of health care: systematic review of the uses, benefits, and limitations of

social media for health communication. J Med Internet Res. 2013 Apr 23; 15 (4): e85.

Ngai, E. W. T., Tao, S. S. C., & Moon, K. K. L. (2015). Social media research: Theories,

constructs, and conceptual frameworks. *International Journal of Information*

Management. https://doi.org/10.1016/j.ijinfomgt.2014.09.004

O. Airhihenbuwa, Bunmi Makinwa, Raf, C. (2000). Toward a new communications

framework for HIV/AIDS. *Journal of Health Communication, 5*(sup1), 101-111.

https://doi.org/10.1080/108107300406820

Obar, J. A., & Wildman, S. S. (2015). Social media definition and the governance challenge: An introduction to the special issue. *SSRN Electronic Journal*. https://doi.org/10.2139/ssrn.2637879

Olufowote, J. O., Aranda, J. S., Wang, G. E., & Liao, D. (2017). Advancing the new communications framework for hiv/Aids: The communicative Constitution of hiv/Aids networks in Tanzania's hiv/Aids Ngo sector. *Studies in Media and Communication*, *5*(1), 79. https://doi.org/10.11114/smc.v5i1.2390

Peter R. Lamptey. (2001). HIV/AIDS Prevention and Care in Resource-Constrained Settings. https://reliefweb.int/sites/reliefweb.int/files/resources/9B91EDF048FD0579C1256E0 0002EB0C8-usaid-hiv-2001.pdf

Rudd, R. (January 28, 2021). What Is Health Literacy? Centers for Disease Control and Prevention. https://www.cdc.gov/healthliteracy/learn/index.html (accessed on 1 April 2021)

Shaddin Dughmi, David Kempe, & Ruixin Qiang. (2016). Persuasion with Limited Communication. https://dl.acm.org/doi/pdf/10.1145/2940716.2940781?casa_token=ktjbtkB4KnsAAA AA:w1t_m78XuLaY6USwtL7vpmTfTmqbGXh-svSWr3OkPMIS8jZc4_WQGdojFhEFDZIdeKETDLLFGPg

Shen, F., Sheer, V. C., & Li, R. (2015). Impact of narratives on persuasion in health communication: A meta-analysis. *Journal of Advertising*, *44*(2), 105-113. https://doi.org/10.1080/00913367.2015.1018467

Statista. (2020, July 14). *Malaysia: Facebook users 2018-2023*.

https://www.statista.com/statistics/490484/number-of-malaysia-facebook-users

Storey, D., Seifert-Ahanda, K., Andaluz, A., Tsoi, B., Matsuki, J. M., & Cutler, B. (2014).
What is health communication and how does it affect the HIV/AIDS continuum of
care? A brief primer and case study from New York City. *JAIDS Journal of Acquired
Immune Deficiency Syndromes, 66*, S241-S249.
https://doi.org/10.1097/qai.0000000000000243

Tabachnick, B. G., & Fidell, L. S. (2012). Using multivariate statistics (6th ed.). In *New York:
Harper and Row.*

Taggart, T., Grewe, M. E., Conserve, D. F., Gliwa, C., & Roman Isler, M. (2015). Social media
and HIV: A systematic review of uses of social media in HIV communication. *Journal of
Medical Internet Research, 17*(11), e248. https://doi.org/10.2196/jmir.4387

Toothaker, L. E., Aiken, L. S., & West, S. G. (1994). Multiple Regression: Testing and
Interpreting Interactions. *The Journal of the Operational Research Society.*
https://doi.org/10.2307/2583960

Tuddenham, S., Koay, W. L., & Sears, C. (2020). HIV, sexual orientation, and gut
microbiome interactions. *Digestive Diseases and Sciences, 65*(3), 800-817.
https://doi.org/10.1007/s10620-020-06110-y

Umeh, D. C. (1997). *undefined.* Africa World Press.

UNAIDS. (1999). Communication Frameworks for HIV/AIDs: A new Direction.
https://www.unaids.org/sites/default/files/media_asset/jc335-commframew_en_1.pdf

UNICEF. (2005). Strategic Communication for Behaviour and Social Change in South Asia.
https://www.faithtoactionnetwork.org/resources/pdf/Strategic_Communication_for_B
ehaviour_and_Social_Change.pdf

WHO. (2000). A Guide for AIDS Programmes Managers. *Information, Education and Communication*.

https://apps.who.int/iris/bitstream/handle/10665/205344/B0224.pdf?sequence=1&is Allowed=y

WHO. (2004). Advocacy Guide on Prev for IDU. http://www.unodc.org/documents/hiv-aids/advocacy%20guide%20on%20prev%20for%20IDU.pdf

WHO. (2017). WHO Strategic Communications Framework for Effective Communications. https://www.who.int/mediacentre/communication-framework.pdf

EXAMPLE OF QUESTIONNAIRES SAMPLE

Part A: Demographics

Instructions: Tick (/) at the relevant field.

1. Gender: Men ( ) Women ( )

2. Age: 18-30 ( ) 30-40 ( ) 40 above ( )

3. Level of education : Sijil Pelajaran Malaysia ( ) Bachelor Degree ( )

   Master's Degree ( ) Doctoral Degrees ( )

4. Household Income: RM 1000 and below ( ), RM1000 to RM2000 ( ), RM2000 to

   RM3000 ( ), RM3000 to RM4000 ( ) and RM5000 above ( )

5. Marital Status: single ( ), married ( ) and divorced ( )

6. Health Status: Healthy ( ) or comorbidities ( )

Part B: Role of Social Media in Seeking and Delivery Information

This section will be focus on the use of social media in seeking and delivery Information
to determine whether there will be relatable or not.

Instructions: Tick (/) at the box provided.

o.	Item	Strongly Disagree	Disagree	Neutral	Agree	Strongly Agree
	You are looking for health issues on social media.					
	You feel social media is an easy platform to get information.					
	You feel the information being disseminated is true and trustworthy.					
	You will refer to health issues on social media.					
	You will refer to accurate information on social media.					
	You agree that the media provides up-to-date information.					

No.	Item					
7.	You will prioritise search on social media for information.					
8.	You are about to share that information with others.					
9.	You agree that chat and discussion on social media provide you with new information					
10.	You agree that chat and discussion on social media are important in finding and receiving information.					
11.	You believe that sharing information through chat and discussion on social media is from the right source.					
12.	You always keep the information available on social media.					
13.	You will refer to information on social media about treatment.					
14.	You will refer to information on social media about HIV / AIDS prevention.					
15.	You agree that social media is an easy platform to get information on prescription drugs, prevention methods, and HIV / AIDS information.					
16.	You know that information on HIV / AIDS is obtained from the ministry of health.					
17.	You know that the health unit will provide relaxing learning on social media.					
18.	You follow the HIV / AIDS prevention program on social media to get the latest information.					
19.	You agree that social media is the best platform for finding information on HIV / AIDS prevention.					
20.	You agree that social media is the best platform for receiving information on HIV / AIDS prevention.					

Part C: Role of Social Media in Persuasion

This section will be focus on the use of social media in persuasion to determine whether there will be relatable or not.

Instructions: Tick (/) at the box provided.

No.	Item	Strongly Disagree	Disagree	Neutral	Agree	Strongly Agree
1.	You are influenced by the spread of information from friends.					
2.	You are easily influenced by the spread of information from family members or relatives,					
3.	You are easily influenced by the invitation of friends through social media.					

.	Social media uses effective persuasion sentences.					
.	The display of information on social media easily influences thinking.					
.	You are affected by ads on social media.					
.	You are affected by the display of graphics on social media.					
.	You trust positive reviews on social media about information.					
.	You will be influenced by ads displayed by legit or correct sources.					
0.	You are easily influenced by the advantages displayed on social media.					
1.	You are easily affected by the adverse effects faced by HIV / AIDS patients through graphic display on social media.					
2.	You often share the post to others.					
3.	You will tell about this post to others.					
4.	You will visit a website or page promoted from ad exposure.					
5.	You will get the details of the ad.					
6.	You can easily trust ads or information on Facebook compared to a spokesperson.					
7.	You believe that the person who is the spokesperson in the Facebook post is the person who is an expert in the field of health.					
8.	You will continue to buy supplements recommended by others on Facebook.					
9.	You participate in the community that helps to invite others to participate in health activities.					
0.	You trust social media ads in the form of detailed and informative descriptions.